Let's Step in 4e

PALIER 2 Niveaux A2 / B1

WORKBOOK 2

This workbook belongs to ....

....

Class ....

School address ....

....

Coordination :
Karine Goyer

Auteurs :
Sandrine Berger
Nicolas Kasprzyk
Sandrine Ladet
Nathalie Vezon

Avec la participation de :
Brenda Marshall

PAPIER RECYCLÉ

Hatier

SOMMAIRE

© Hatier, avril 2008 - ISBN 978-2-218-93052-2

1 GET READY!

Sounds: L'accent tonique

En anglais, dans chaque mot de deux syllabes ou plus, une syllabe est plus accentuée.
Ex.: *a reporter; a **news**paper* 45

45 **Listen to these words and underline the stressed syllable.**

• *re-por-ter* • *pho-to-gra-pher* • *e-di-tor* • *news-a-gent* • *news-rea-der* • *sound re-cor-dist*

◆ **Comment.** He's a reporter.

a. What are the jobs of these famous people?

Doisneau and Sieff Harry Roselmack Jerry Bruckheimer Leonardo DiCaprio Marilyn Monroe Steven Spielberg and Tim Burton	an actor an actress directors a newsreader photographers a producer

1. ....
....
2. ....
....
3. ....
4. ....
5. ....
6. ....

→ Observe et réfléchis

1. Charlie Chaplin was an actor. 2. Yann Arthus-Bertrand is a photographer.
3. Steven Spielberg and Tim Burton are directors.

• Souligne le verbe, et entoure les articles quand il y en a.

Que trouve-t-on devant les noms de métier ?

Dans les phrases 1 et 2 : ☐ un article défini ☐ un article indéfini ☐ rien

Dans la phrase 3 : ☐ un article défini ☐ un article indéfini ☐ rien

REMEMBER

• Devant les noms de métier au singulier, j'utilise ....

• J'utilise ...... devant un nom commençant par un « son voyelle ».

Ex. : ....

• J'utilise ...... devant un nom commençant par un « son consonne ».

Ex. : ....

• Devant des noms de métier au pluriel, je n'utilise pas ....

Ex. : ....

Find out the job of these famous French people: Thierry Henry and Franck Ribéry / Jenifer and Lorie / Claire Chazal / Jean Dujardin / Luc Besson

....

....

....

....

....

b. What about you?

What would you like to be? What wouldn't you like to be?

....

....

2 STEP FORWARD!

MP3 A. Listen and comment.

How **is** a newspaper **made**?

a. Put the pictures in the correct order (from 1 to 4). Then listen to check your answers.

......

......

......

......

b. Now recap to say how a newspaper is made, using the expressions given below.

The articles and the best photos	*(deliver)*	into lorries.
The pages	*(print)*	by the editor.
The newspapers	*(load)*	to newsagents'.
The newspapers	*(choose)*	with printing presses.

The article is written by a reporter. ....

....

....

→ Observe et réfléchis

1. The article is written by a reporter. 2. The newspapers are delivered to newsagents'.

- Le groupe verbal se compose de .... et d'un verbe au. ....

Dans ces phrases, le sujet fait-il l'action exprimée par le verbe ? ☐ oui ☐ non
Ces phrases sont donc à la voix ☐ active. ☐ passive.

REMEMBER

- J'utilise la voix passive quand le sujet de la phrase ne fait pas l'action exprimée par le verbe.
- La voix passive se forme avec l'auxiliaire .... suivi du .... au ....

Ex. : ....

⚠ **Attention !**
Quand le verbe est régulier, au participe passé il prend la terminaison ....
Quand il est irrégulier, il faut l'apprendre par cœur (voir liste pp. 172-173).
On peut ou non choisir de mentionner le complément d'agent (celui qui fait l'action).
Il est introduit par ***by***.

Ex. : ....

3 IN THE NEWS The release of "The 11th Hour"

A. Before you listen.

Look at the pictures and make hypotheses. Tick what you expect to hear.

1. The document you're going to listen to is … ☐ an extract from a film.
☐ an extract from the TV News. ☐ an interview of a famous actor.

2. It is about … ☐ the release of Leonardo DiCaprio's new film.
☐ an eco-movement meeting with DiCaprio. ☐ the release of DiCaprio's eco-site.

3. The poster shows that it is about … ☐ the story of mankind.
☐ the story of an adventurer travelling round the world. ☐ human impact upon planet Earth.

Step 1

B. Listen.

a. Listen and check your answers above. Circle the right answers.

b. Listen again and fill in the grid.

Title of the film	....	
Producer	....	
Narrator	....	
Director	☐ Leonardo DiCaprio ☐ Al Gore ☐ Leila and Nadia Conners	
It is about ...	☐ ecological problems. ☐ solutions for the environment.	☐ the end of the world. ☐ the story of a famous scientist.

c. Are these sentences true (T) or false (F)? Justify your answers.

1. Many scientists and experts have taken part in this film. ☐ T ☐ F

....

2. The planet's problems are due to human activity. ☐ T ☐ F

....

3. The film is about the end of planet Earth. ☐ T ☐ F

....

4. The film is pessimistic: it says there aren't any solutions. ☐ T ☐ F

....

5. Leonardo DiCaprio has got an eco-site. ☐ T ☐ F

....

4 MAKE IT YOURS!

◆ Present the poster of a film to the class.

Choose a film which has just been released (cinema or DVD) and describe the poster to the class. Then say who the film is directed by, produced by, who plays in it, where it is set...
You can fill in the grid below to help you.

Title of the film	....
Producer	....
Director	....
Script	....
Actors	....

1 GET READY!

◆ **Look and comment.** At that time, **there were** no...

→ Observe et réfléchis

At that time there were no computers.

• Souligne le verbe et entoure le sujet.

• Quel est le verbe utilisé ? .... À quel temps est-il ? ....

Quel est l'élément qui justifie l'emploi de ce temps ? ....

• Pourquoi n'a-t-on pas utilisé ***was*** ? (Regarde le nom en fin de phrase pour t'aider.)

....

• *There were no computers* signifie : ☐ Il y avait des ordinateurs. ☐ Il n'y avait pas d'ordinateurs.

REMEMBER

• Pour poser l'existence de quelque chose à un moment du ....

on utilise l'expression *there* + ... conjugué au ....

• On accorde ce verbe en fonction de l'élément qui suit (singulier ou pluriel).

Ex. : ....

What about you?

You went to a birthday party but you didn't enjoy it very much. Explain why.

A few ideas

• no CDs • no decorations • only four guests • no sweets • too many parents...

....

....

....

2 STEP FORWARD!

Sounds: **Les mots accentués**

Dans les phrases, les mots ne sont pas prononcés avec la même force.

Ex.: *The **microphone** was **invented** in **1887**.*

46

46 **Listen carefully and repeat.**

It was **invented** for **speakers** to be **heard** in **large places**.
The **word "television"** was **first used** in **1900**.

→ Observe et réfléchis

The microphone was invented in 1887.

• Souligne le sujet de la phrase et entoure la forme verbale.

La forme verbale est constituée de l'auxiliaire .... conjugué au ....

et d'un verbe au ....

• Le sujet de la phrase ☐ est à l'origine de l'action exprimée par le verbe.
☐ n'est pas à l'origine de l'action exprimée par le verbe ; il en « subit » l'action, il est « passif » par rapport à l'action.

• L'inventeur est-il mentionné ? ....

• À la voix passive, l'élément à l'origine de l'action exprimée par le verbe n'est pas nécessairement mentionné.

REMEMBER

• À la voix ...., le sujet de la phrase n'est pas à l' ....
de l'action exprimée par le verbe.

La voix passive se forme à l'aide de l'auxiliaire .... suivi d'un verbe au ....

Ex. : ....

B. What about you?

You wanted to help your parents redecorate your room but everything was finished when you came back from holiday. Explain what was done, using the verbs below.

repaint • change • hang • remove • replace by a new one

1. The walls ....
2. The carpet ....
3. New curtains ....
4. The old computer desk ....
5. The posters ....

3 A SURVEY Waste yesterday and today

B. Listen.

a. Listen once and write down ten words you've heard.

....

....

....

b. Number the pictures as you hear the situations.

c. Listen again and match.

Your soda bottle •	• were transformed into a material used for running tracks.
Your sandwich •	• is composted into fertilizer.
The brown bag •	• is transformed into a kitchen work surface.
245 million tons of garbage •	• was thrown away.
Athletic shoes •	• is turned into paper for textbooks.

d. Recap, using the following elements.

was thrown • *the Environmental Protection Agency* • *can be recycled* • *are composted* • *are turned* • *was invited* • *are transformed* • *no trash*

Alan Jones is a member of .... He ....
to tell a class about rubbish in the USA.

He explains how garbage ....; for example plastic bottles
.... into kitchen work surface, sandwiches .... into
fertilizers and brown bags .... into paper.

He also adds that in 2005 in the USA, 245 million tons of garbage .... away and that it would be a great improvement to recycle as much as possible and live in a world with ....

1 GET READY!

Sounds: ***whose, who***

Il faut faire attention à la prononciation de *whose* [hu:z] et de *who* [hu:].
Le *w-* ne se prononce pas et le *-h-* est expiré. 47

47 **Listen carefully and repeat.**

Whose is it? • Who's in here? • Whose are those? • Who are they?

◆ **Listen.** **Whose** copybook is it? It's Laura**'s**.

a. Anticipate.
Look at the pictures in your textbook and write down the words you expect to hear.

....

....

48 **b. Listen once and tick the question you hear.**

☐ Who are they? ☐ Whose are they?

48 **c. Listen again and match the objects to their owners (*leurs possesseurs*).**

fountain pen

Tom

ruler

Laura

calculator

→ Observe et réfléchis

1. Whose copybook is it? 2. It's Laura's copybook.

• Entoure le **mot interrogatif** de la question et souligne le mot qui le suit.

Il s'agit d'un .... commun.

Entoure le nom propre de la réponse. Par quoi est-il suivi ? ....

• *Whose copybook is it?* signifie « .... est ce cahier ? »

• *It's Laura's copybook.* signifie « C'est le cahier .... Laura. »

En anglais, ... marque le lien de possession entre Laura et le cahier. On l'appelle le **génitif**.

Que remarques-tu sur l'ordre des mots en anglais et en français ? ....

REMEMBER

• Pour demander .... appartient quelque chose, j'utilise le mot interrogatif .... suivi directement d'un .... commun.

Ex. : ....

• Pour dire que quelqu'un possède quelque chose, j'utilise le génitif « .... » qui se place entre le possesseur et l'objet possédé.

Ex. : ....

The dog in your host family has stolen a lot of things in the neighbours' gardens. Help the father find their owners.

1. The father – Whose .... do you think it is?
   You – Um! I think it's .... 's.
2. The father – ....
   You – ....
3. The father – ....
   You – ....

2 STEP FORWARD!

→ Observe et réfléchis

1. Do you know the name of the chemical **which** is extremely polluting?
2. Do you know the name of the politician **who** won the Nobel Prize?

• Les deux phrases sont des phrases complexes (c'est-à-dire faites de deux propositions), reliées par un **pronom relatif**.

• « pronom » signifie « qui remplace un nom » et pour savoir quel pronom employer il faut :
– regarder **quel nom est remplacé** (c'est l'antécédent, « celui qui est placé avant »),
– déterminer **quelle fonction** a le pronom dans la seconde proposition (sujet, complément d'objet...).

• *chemical* est un nom qui fait référence ☐ à une chose. ☐ à une personne.
• *politician* est un nom qui fait référence ☐ à une chose. ☐ à une personne.

• ***who*** et ***which*** ont la fonction de .... dans la seconde proposition.

REMEMBER

• ***who*** et ***which*** sont des .... Ils servent à relier en une seule phrase deux propositions. Ils ont la fonction de .... dans la deuxième proposition.

• ***who*** a pour antécédent un nom propre ou un nom commun faisant référence à une ....

Ex. : ....

• ***which*** a pour antécédent un nom propre ou un nom commun faisant référence à une ....

Ex. : ....

You're talking about a girl you met at a party last Saturday night.

Do you know the name of the girl .... was in blue? No, not the one .... was wearing those horrible shoes! Yes! The one .... was a bit shy! She gave me her mobile number! And I wrote it on a piece of paper but I've lost it!!! She had a lovely name .... reminded me of an actress. Yes! It was Sharon!!

B. Listen and answer. Say the name scientists give to the rise in temperature of the Earth.

49 **Listen to a radio game and try to answer before the contestants.**

☐ Katrina	☐ polar bear	☐ global warming	☐ hurricane
☐ el Niño	☐ coral reef	☐ Yann Arthus-Bertrand	☐ storm

→ Observe et réfléchis

1. Give the name of an enormous white animal whose habitat is seriously threatened by climate change!
2. What's the name Ø scientists give to the rise in temperature of the Earth?

- Dans la phrase complexe 1, les deux propositions sont reliées par le pronom relatif ....
- Dans la phrase complexe 2, Ø indique une absence de pronom.
- Dans la phrase 1, quel mot suit directement *whose* ? ....

Il s'agit d'un .... commun.

– *whose* a une fonction de ☐ COD ☐ complément du nom dans la deuxième proposition.

– *whose* signifie « .... »

- Dans la phrase 2, quel mot suit directement Ø ? ....

Il s'agit d'un .... commun.

– Ø a une fonction de ☐ COD ☐ complément du nom dans la deuxième proposition.

REMEMBER

- ***whose*** signifie « .... ». Il est complément du nom de la deuxième proposition.

Ex. : ....

- Ø signifie « .... » quand il est COD de la deuxième proposition.

Ex. : ....

- **Remarque :** On n'utilise « Ø » que pour les explications grammaticales. On ne trouve jamais ce symbole dans un document en anglais.

You attended a conference on climate change at your pen friend's school. You're talking about it with your English teacher.

I really liked the Biology teacher .... explanations were very clear. The documents ..... she commented on were very interesting and the examples .... she chose were very captivating.

3 AN ARTICLE FROM A WEBSITE How climate change puts animals in danger

Read.

a. Read the text once and circle the correct answers.

The document is **a press article / a web page** on **climate change / sustainable development**.

b. Read and tick the correct translation.

1. increase ☐ *augmentation* ☐ *diminution*
2. support ☐ *soutenir* ☐ *démolir*
3. lead an action ☐ *dénoncer une action* ☐ *mener une action*
4. wilderness ☐ *région sauvage* ☐ *région peuplée*

c. Read again and say if the following statements are true (T) or false (F). Justify by quoting from the text.

1. The effects of greenhouse gases are destroying the habitat of pandas. ☐ T ☐ F

....

2. Polar bears hunt for food on the ice fields. ☐ T ☐ F

....

3. Climate change only affects human life. ☐ T ☐ F

....

4. WWF's mission is to accelerate the degradation of the environment. ☐ T ☐ F

....

4 MAKE IT YOURS!

◆ Write an essay.

You're writing an essay on WWF. Make sentences using the following information and "who", "which", "whose". Give your opinion on WWF.

<u>WWF:</u> a charity
<u>Date of creation:</u> 1961
<u>Panda logo:</u> symbol of conservation and sustainable development
<u>First mission:</u> protect the world's species and their habitats
<u>Mission today:</u> conserve the world's biodiversity; reduce pollution

....
....
....
....
....
....
....
....
....
....

1. Read the texts, look at the pictures and fill in the grid.

	Good for our planet	Bad for our planet
Sources of energy		
Technologies, inventions or discoveries		
Consequences		

2. Do this word search, then learn these words linked to the environment.

T	U	D	M	B	O	L	D	S	G	G	C	X	Q	K	B	Y
H	N	F	F	L	I	U	Z	I	B	J	F	U	D	G	H	T
G	R	E	E	N	H	O	U	S	E	E	F	F	E	C	T	I
E	A	S	M	I	W	F	D	W	L	Y	D	G	F	A	W	C
G	F	S	I	N	L	K	Q	E	G	R	A	S	O	U	Y	I
M	H	K	O	Q	O	K	Z	R	G	S	C	E	R	W	J	R
A	Q	Y	Y	L	Y	R	E	C	E	R	L	H	E	W	Q	T
C	U	F	L	J	I	N	I	M	Z	U	A	I	S	C	D	C
L	C	R	Z	Q	E	N	I	V	T	H	Q	D	T	K	L	E
O	B	Q	W	R	L	S	E	I	N	K	Y	C	A	Q	V	L
V	K	E	A	W	S	T	N	L	R	E	S	O	T	B	S	E
Z	Z	L	W	I	W	Q	Y	F	I	Y	J	L	I	K	L	L
R	O	H	O	V	Q	P	O	L	L	U	T	I	O	N	R	E
S	J	N	L	G	N	I	T	U	L	L	O	P	N	O	N	S
L	S	Q	D	E	J	Y	J	M	R	S	L	F	W	G	L	U

BIODEGRADABLE
DEFORESTATION
ELECTRICITY
ENVIRONMENT
GAS EMISSIONS
GASOLINE
GREENHOUSE EFFECT
NON POLLUTING
POLLUTION
SOLAR ENERGY

3. Write.

Now write a few lines to say which invention or new technology you like best and say why. (You can use the words from the word search.)

. . . .

. . . .

. . . .

. . . .

. . . .

. . . .

. . . .

. . . .

DVD

A Greenpeace campaign

1. Watch the video without the soundtrack.

a. Observe carefully and pick out words that have to do with the video.

☐ river ☐ ice ☐ animals ☐ baby ☐ old man
☐ trees ☐ glacier [glæ'sɪə] ☐ cities ☐ factories* ☐ teenager

* factories: *usines.*

b. Match and make sentences.

The baby •
The glacier •

• is getting cold.
• is melting.
• is becoming an old man.

....

....

....

2. Watch the video with the soundtrack.

a. Complete with words from the soundtrack.

The glacier is ...., so the sea level is ....

As a consequence, ... of .... will be ....

b. Use the following words to sum up the message of the video.

IF...	THEN THE WORLD...
don't / against / we / climate change / take action	dramatically / change / will

If..,

then the world ....

c. Fill in the grid.

Type of document: ☐ a TV series ☐ a report ☐ an ad ☐ a film ☐ a documentary

Organization: ....

Final slogan: ....

d. Think about another slogan for this video sequence.

....

1. First, go to the following website to find out the meaning of these words and fill in the grid.

http://www.recyclezone.org.uk/iz_wastewords.aspx

recycling	
3Rs	
rubbish	
reuse	
litter	
greenhouse gas	

2. Reducing waste.

a. What is waste?

Go to the following website and complete.

http://ollierecycles.com/uk/html/waste_what.html

Definition: ....

Problems: ....

....

b. How can you reduce waste at home?

Go to the following website and find out what you can reuse or recycle. Then fill in the grid.

http://www.planetpals.com/EDrecyclethings/recyclefacts.html

Items that can be recycled	
Items that can be reused	
Items to be disposed of properly and carefully	

c. Recycling in British schools.

Go to the following website and answer the question.

http://www.recyclingconsortium.org.uk/teachers/recycling_procedures/bristolsecondary.htm

What can be recycled?

....

....

d. Have fun!

Go to the following website and do the rubbish challenge!

http://www.recyclezone.org.uk/fz_challenge.aspx

1. Word building.

a. Here are nouns you studied through Unit 4. Match each noun to the corresponding verb.

destruction •	• pollute
deforestation •	• destroy
pollution •	• degrade
degradation •	• deforest
emission •	• invent
invention •	• emit

b. Can you find the nouns corresponding to these two words?

conserve: .... implicate: ....

2. Let's talk about jobs!

a. Look at this word, "photographer": photograph + -er = photographer (job)

root (*racine*) suffix

b. Do the same with the following words and give the name of other jobs.

root		suffix		jobs
garden	+	....	=	....
report	+	....	=	....
paint	+	....	=	....
teach	+	....	=	....
write	+	....	=	....
join	+	....	=	....

3. Word building.

Look at the compound word "wildlife" and find out how it is made:

wild + life = wildlife

sauvage vie la faune et la flore

a. Take one word from each box and write a compound word for each translation.

NUCLEAR LITTER BOOK TIN BLACK	SHELF OPENER PLANT BOARD BIN

1. .... = *une centrale nucléaire*
2. .... = *un tableau noir*
3. .... = *une poubelle*
4. .... = *un ouvre-boîte*
5. .... = *une étagère (à livres)*

b. Now complete the following sentences using one of the compound words.

1. I want to open a tin of baked beans, can you give me the ....
2. Please put away your books on the ....
3. Go to the .... and write the date.
4. Can you throw your rubbish in the ...., please?
5. I visited a .... that produces electricity.

53 **1. Listen to these words, find out where the stressed syllable is, then fill in the grid.**

degradation • hurricane • climate • wilderness • sustainable • ozone • politician • responsible

Oo	Ooo	oOoo	ooOo
....	....	....	....
....	....	....	....

54 **2. Listen to the following words. Do you hear the sound [aɪ] or [eɪ]? Tick the right answer, then repeat.**

	climate	danger	teenager	survival	rely	great	recycle	patient
[aɪ]								
[eɪ]								

3. A hidden message.

Read and write this sentence in English.

[huːz kɒpɪbʊk ɪz ɪt]

....

UNIT 4 Let's recap!

1. Lis les phrases suivantes et souligne les mots importants, ceux qui sont accentués.

a. The telephone was invented by Graham Bell.
b. The weather report is read by Miranda.

2 x 1 point
...... / 2 points

2. Fais une liste pour organiser la fête d'anniversaire d'un(e) ami(e) en précisant par qui sont faites les différentes tâches.

The cakes .... (*bake*) by Julian and Amy. The drinks .... (*buy*) by Sue and Jim and the CDs .... (*bring*) by Lucy and John.

3 x 1 point
...... / 3 points

3. Tu dois faire un bref exposé en classe sur l'invention du morse. Prépare ton intervention à l'aide des expressions qui te sont données.

a. The first American telegraph / build / Samuel Finley Breese Morse / around 1835.

....

b. A dots-and-spaces code / use / for the letters of the alphabet.

....

c. The first telegraphic message / send / on May 24, 1844 from Washington D.C. to Baltimore.

....

d. Long distance communications / revolutionized / thanks to Morse.

....

4 x 2 points
...... / 8 points

4. Complète cette présentation d'un photographe célèbre à l'aide de pronoms relatifs.

Yann Arthus-Bertrand is a photographer .... aerial photographs invite us to think about the Earth's evolution and the future of its inhabitants. He is at the head of GoodPlanet, ... is a non-profit organization .... aim is to raise public awareness of our world's issues and promote sustainable development.

3 x 1 point
...... / 3 points

5. Quel est l'équivalent anglais des mots et expressions ci-dessous ?

prévisions météorologiques : ....
sortie (d'un film) : ....
télécommande : ....
téléphone portable : ....

recycler : ....
effet de serre : ....
gaspillage : ....
déchets : ....

8 x 0,5 point
...... / 4 points

Pas de problème. C'est moyen. Il faut que je révise.

Total : ...... / 20 points

1 GET READY!

◆ Look and comment.

They **have** clean**ed** the park.

Look at the pictures and write what they have done.

Ex.: *Ron has picked up the cans.*

....

....

....

....

→ Observe et réfléchis

1. They have repaired the basketball hoop.
2. They have built a fence.

- Souligne les groupes verbaux dans les phrases ci-dessus.
- Dans ces phrases, l'énonciateur exprime ☐ une action en cours de réalisation. ☐ le bilan d'une action.

Le verbe est conjugué au ☐ *present perfect.* ☐ prétérit.

REMEMBER

- Quand je veux exprimer le bilan présent d'une action passée, j'emploie le ....

L'auxiliaire « .... » est conjugué au .... , suivi du .... du verbe.

Your class is on a school trip in England. The English school has organized a sports tournament. Comment on these pictures you're going to put on the trip blog. Say what has happened.

1. ....

2. ....

3. ....

2 STEP FORWARD!

Sounds: La prononciation de *th-*

En position initiale, le *th-* se prononce :
- [ð] pour la plupart des mots grammaticaux (déterminants, adverbes, pronoms…). Ex.: *the, this*
- [θ] pour la plupart des noms, des adjectifs et des verbes. Ex.: *themes, think*
- [t] dans certains cas particuliers. Ex.: *Thames, Thomas, Thailand.*

55

55 **Listen to the following words. Do you hear [ð], [θ], [t]? Tick the correct answer.**

	that	Thames	there	theatre	Thomas	three	thanks	thousand	them
[ð]									
[θ]									
[t]									

A. Listen. I have **just** received some good news.

MP3 **a. Listen to this conversation and fill in the grid.**

	Person who is answering	Person who is calling
Name		
Phone number		

MP3 **b. Listen again and tick the correct answers.**

1. Mr Jones has just ☐ gone to work.
   ☐ gone to the theatre.

2. Mr Black and Mr Jones want to help ☐ ChildLine's charity.
   ☐ Centrepoint's charity.

3. To collect money, they have organized ☐ a football match.
   ☐ a charity race along the River Thames.

4. ☐ Chelsea Football Club
   ☐ Arsenal Football Club
   has just decided to give money to the charity.

5. The club's chairman has just decided to give ☐ £ 300,000.
   ☐ £ 3,000.

6. A few players have promised ☐ to send money too.
   ☐ to be present at the race.

→ Observe et réfléchis

1. Mr Jones has just left.
2. The Football club has just decided to give money to the charity.

- Souligne le groupe verbal et entoure l'adverbe.
- Quelle est la forme verbale dans les deux phrases ci-dessus ? ....

Où se place l'adverbe dans les deux phrases ? ....

Cet adverbe souligne
☐ que l'événement a eu lieu il y a longtemps.
☐ que l'événement vient de se passer.

REMEMBER

L'adverbe .... employé avec le .... présente une action qui vient de .... et renforce l'idée de bilan.

Mr Jones is leaving the supermarket. He's just done some shopping for the charity race.

4 chocolate bars
5 cereal bars
2 bottles of water
1 tee-shirt
1 pair of shorts
1 pair of trainers
1 waterproof coat
2 energetic drinks

Cross on the list below what he hasn't bought and write down what he has just bought.

☐ a tee-shirt ☐ shorts ☐ trainers ☐ a waterproof coat

☐ chocolate bars ☐ bottles of water ☐ cereal bars ☐ energetic drinks

....

....

....

....

3 ANNOUNCEMENTS At the airport

A. Before you listen.

a. Complete these sentences with the verbs below in the present perfect.

organize • buy • raise • have

1. The pupils from Ross High School .... an Open Day.
2. They .... a lot of money.
3. They .... a lot of school equipment.
4. They .... a school trip to bring the equipment to a school in Africa.

b. Write the following words under each picture.

customs • landing • taking off • checking • boarding • duty free shops

....

....

....

....

....

....

B. Listen.

a. Listen to the dialogue and tick the right answer.

1. Josh and his class are going to ☐ Kenya. ☐ Tanzania.
2. Flight to Mombasa: boarding has just ☐ started. ☐ finished.
3. Josh and his class ☐ have been through customs. ☐ are getting their passports ready.

b. Listen. Are these sentences true (T) or false (F)? Justify your answers.

1. Josh has just been to the duty free shops. ☐ T ☐ F

....

2. Boarding for the flight to Nairobi has just begun. ☐ T ☐ F

....

3. Sam and Thomas have just gone to the shops. ☐ T ☐ F

....

c. Now complete these sentences, using the following verbs (use the present perfect with "just").

announce • begin • go to the toilets

1. The steward .... the boarding for the flight to Mombasa.
2. Josh can't go shopping because boarding ....
3. The class is going to be late because Sam and Thomas ....

4 MAKE IT YOURS!

◆ Write.

Josh is now back from his trip. He is waiting for his luggage at London airport and he's calling his mum at home. He's telling her what he has just done. Write their conversation.

A few ideas

go through the customs • get one of my bags • (teacher) go to phone the bus driver • (bus) arrive • (best friend) go to the toilets

....

....

....

....

....

....

....

....

....

....

....

....

....

1 GET READY!

→ Observe et réfléchis

1. – Have you got **any** brown sugar?
2. – No, I haven't got any.
3. I've only got **some** white sugar.

Dans la phrase ☐ 1 ☐ 2 ☐ 3, l'énonciateur dit qu'il n'a que du sucre blanc.
Dans la phrase ☐ 1 ☐ 2 ☐ 3, l'énonciateur demande s'il y a du sucre roux.
Dans la phrase ☐ 1 ☐ 2 ☐ 3, l'énonciateur dit qu'il n'a pas de sucre roux.

REMEMBER

• ***some*** et ***any*** s'emploient pour des quantités indéterminées.

• ***any***

- s'emploie dans des phrases .... pour demander s'il y a telle chose.
- s'emploie dans des phrases .... pour dire qu'il n'y en a pas.

• ***some***

s'emploie dans des phrases .... pour dire qu'il y en a.

• Remarque : ***some*** peut également s'employer dans des phrases interrogatives :
– pour proposer quelque chose : *Would you like some tea?*
– pour demander quelque chose quand on sait qu'il y en a : *May I have some sugar, please?*
(Je sais qu'il y a du sucre, je demande si je peux en avoir.)

◆ What about you? Have you got **any** milk?

Your head teacher is organizing a party for a charity. But there are still many things missing. Check on the list what you have at home. Then, write an e-mail to your classmates, tell them about the items you have got or haven't got at home and ask them what they have got for the party.

The Head Teachers' list

- ☐ CD
- ☐ paper napkins
- ☐ confetti
- ☐ streamers
- ☐ paper hats
- ☐ personal items for the car boot sales: rollerblades, a jigsaw puzzle, a toy train, a doll...
- ☐ wall decorations
- ☐ paper cups
- ☐ chairs
- ☐ drinking straws

....
....
....
....
....
....

2 STEP FORWARD!

Sounds: ***have*** **forme faible [əv] et forme pleine [hæv]** 56

56 **Listen and tick the correct answer.**

	1	2	3	4
[hæv/hæz]	☐	☐	☐	☐
[əv/əz]	☐	☐	☐	☐

A. Look and comment. We **have already organized** the concert but we **haven't performed yet**.

You need to get ready for the book fair in May. Here is a list of what your class has done and hasn't done yet.
Ask your classmates if you can help them.

Ex.: *I see you haven't put any posters in the streets yet. Would you like me to help you?*

Book fair check list

- ☑ contact the local paper for the publication of an article
- ☐ put some posters in the streets
- ☐ send invitations to the town councillors
- ☐ contact the parents' associations
- ☑ call the fire brigade
- ☐ rent or borrow stalls
- ☑ make a list of the participants (publishers, distributors, wholesalers...)

....
....
....
....
....
....
....
....

→ Observe et réfléchis

We haven't planned the football matches yet.

- Souligne la base verbale et encadre l'auxiliaire.
- Quelle est la forme verbale employée dans cette phrase ? ....

Cette phrase est une phrase ☐ affirmative. ☐ négative. ☐ interrogative.

Choisis la bonne traduction : ☐ Nous avons déjà planifié les matches de football.
☐ Nous n'avons pas encore planifié les matches de football.

REMEMBER

- Quand j'utilise ***yet*** dans des phrases ...., il se place .... et se traduit par ....
- ***yet*** s'emploie avec le ....
- J'emploie ***yet*** pour constater qu'une tâche, une action n'est pas encore .... (mais elle va être faite, elle est prévue, programmée).

Step 2

You are doing your homework when you receive an e-mail from your best friend asking you to come and help him / her. Write him / her an e-mail saying you can't because you haven't finished yet the things you have to do.

A few ideas

(finish) Maths exercise • (write) book report • (do) History project • (learn) poem

....

....

....

....

....

....

B. Listen. Have you chosen your topic yet?

57 **a. Listen to the conversation and tick the correct answers (there are several correct answers).**

The pupils want to make
☐ Christmas cards. ☐ Mother's Day cards. ☐ Birthday cards.
☐ Valentine's Day cards. ☐ Wedding Day cards. ☐ Thank You cards.

57 **b. Listen and choose the correct statement.**

1. ☐ The pupils haven't started the drawings yet.
   ☐ The pupils have just started the drawings.
2. ☐ The school has already done something on the theme of Christmas.
   ☐ The school has never done anything on the theme of Christmas.

57 **c. Listen to this passage again and fill in the blanks.**

I think we should make Christmas cards, in previous fund-raising events the school .... already ...., we .... never .... anything on the theme of Christmas. Miss, ... you .... to Sentebale about our ideas .... ?

→ Observe et réfléchis

Have they started the drawings yet?

- Souligne la base verbale et encadre l'auxiliaire.
- Cette phrase est une phrase ☐ affirmative. ☐ négative. ☐ interrogative.
- Traduis : « Ont-ils .... commencé les dessins ? »

REMEMBER

• Quand ***yet*** s'utilise dans des phrases .... il se traduit par .... et il sert à demander si une tâche, une action, qui était prévue, a déjà été faite, ou non.

• ***yet*** peut s'utiliser dans des phrases .... et ....

⚠ Quelle que soit la forme de la phrase, ***yet*** se place toujours à ....

You are at home and you want to go and help your friends at the book fair organized for Sentebale. Your mother asks you if you have done your chores*.
Imagine the dialogue between you and your mother.

*chores: *tâches ménagères*

A few ideas

tidy your room • take the dustbin out • walk the dog

....

....

....

....

....

....

....

3 AN INTERVIEW Running for a charity

B. Listen.

a. Listen to the dialogue and answer the following questions.

1. How many people are talking? ☐ one ☐ two ☐ three
2. Can you give their names?

....

3. Lucy sounds ☐ excited. ☐ worried. ☐ sad.
4. Have the boys practised running blindfolded? ....
5. Have they bought their tee-shirts yet? ....

b. Two of the characters have a dog. Fill in the grid.

Name of the character	....	Teddy
Name of the dog	Nicky	....

1 GET READY!

◆ Listen.

When did they hire the bikes?
How long did they rent them?

a. Anticipate.

Look at the picture and write down 5 words you expect to hear.

....

58 **b. Listen.**

What time did they hire the bikes? What time did they give them back? So, how long did they rent them? Listen and fill in the grid.

	... rented the bikes ...	*... gave them back ...*	*... so they rented them for ...*
The Jones	☐ at 10 o'clock ☐ at 6 o'clock	☐ at 6 o'clock ☐ at 8 o'clock	☐ 6 hours ☐ 8 hours

c. Now ask your classmate questions to correct the grid.

Ex.: YOU – *What time did the Jones rent the bikes?*
YOUR CLASSMATE – *They rented them at ...*

→ Observe et réfléchis

He rented a bike at ten o'clock so he cycled for eight hours.

• Dans la phrase, relève une heure précise. ....

Est-elle précédée d'une préposition ? Si oui, laquelle ? ....

• Dans la phrase, relève une durée. ....

Est-elle précédée d'une préposition ? Si oui, laquelle ? ....

• Associe l'expression anglaise à sa traduction.

at two o'clock •   • pendant deux heures
for two hours •   • à deux heures

REMEMBER

• Pour dire « il est 6 heures », je dis *It's six* ....

• Pour dire « à 6 heures », j'utilise la préposition « .... »

• Pour dire le temps qu'a duré une action, j'utilise « *hours* » ou tout autre unité de temps précédée de la préposition « .... »

Jessica is at school, back from a school trip. She phones her mother. Complete the conversation.

JESSICA – Hi mum! We're back, at last!

HER MOTHER – Hi honey! Are you okay? What time did you arrive?

JESSICA – .... 3:30! The ferry was late and we missed the train!

We were due to arrive ...... 1 ....!

HER MOTHER – Oh, so you travelled ...... 11 ....!

JESSICA – Yeah! But I'm okay! We had a great time on the train!

HER MOTHER – Good to hear you sweetie! See you tonight!

2 STEP FORWARD!

Sounds: **Les diphtongues [eɪ] et [eə]**

Il faut bien faire la différence entre la diphtongue [eɪ] et la diphtongue [eə].
Ex.: *trade* [eɪ] ; *fair* [eə]

59

59 **Listen to the following words. Do you hear [eɪ] or [eə]? Tick the correct answer.**

	container	trainer	wear	their	stay	share	paper	sustainable	care
[eɪ]									
[eə]									

A. Listen. How long has she used reusable containers?

a. Anticipate by matching the words to their definitions.

lunchbox •	• a box in which pupils put their food for lunch at school
sustainable •	• made to minimize environmental damage
aluminium foil •	• produced without using chemicals
organic •	• the activity of buying and selling products to poor countries at fair prices
fair trade •	• metal sheets as thin as paper (for food)

MP3 **b. Now listen and tick the question you hear.**

☐ How long have you had them?
☐ How long have you been in this school?

MP3 **c. Now listen again and complete these sentences.**

1. Deb has been in this school ☐ since last Monday. ☐ for six months.
2. She has used containers ☐ for ages. ☐ since she saw a program on TV.
3. She has had her trainers ☐ since she discovered a fair trade fashion shop. ☐ for two weeks.
4. She hasn't had a bath ☐ for ages. ☐ since she decided to stop washing.

→ Observe et réfléchis

1. How long have you used containers?
2. I've used containers for years, since 2001 actually.

• Dans la question (1), entoure l'expression interrogative et souligne le groupe verbal.
Dans la réponse (2), souligne le groupe verbal.

• Dans la question et la réponse, les verbes sont conjugués au ....

Cette forme permet de faire un .... au présent.

• Dans la question, l'énonciateur demande
☐ quand la personne utilise des boîtes plastiques.
☐ depuis combien de temps la personne utilise des boîtes plastiques.

• Dans la réponse, repère les prépositions précédant le complément de temps et coche.

« .... » est suivi ☐ d'une référence à un moment précis. ☐ d'une durée.

« .... » est suivi ☐ d'une référence à un moment précis. ☐ d'une durée.

REMEMBER

• Pour faire un .... au présent, j'utilise le ....

• Il y a deux possibilités pour traduire « depuis » :

– « .... » est suivi d'un moment précis ou d'une date *(December, last summer, Tuesday 12th, I was born ...)*

– « .... » est suivi d'une durée *(a week, two minutes, three years ...)*

Remarque :
Pour traduire ces phrases en français, j'utilise le présent :
*How long **have** you **used** containers?* Depuis combien de temps **utilises**-tu ... ?
***I've used** containers for years.* J'**utilise** ...
***I've used** containers since 2001.* J'**utilise** ...

• **Say in English:**

depuis deux semaines : ....

depuis des semaines : ....

depuis janvier : ....

depuis 2007 : ....

• You're in your twinned school in London and you've met a new pupil. Tell your friend about him / her, using the expressions below with "for" or "since".

Ex.: *be in London / two weeks* → *He's been in London for two weeks.*

be a vegetarian / one year • use refillable ink cartridges / 2007 • have a bike / last summer

....

....

....

....

....

....

B. Write. How long have you been recycling?

a. After lunch, Bob meets his best friend Paul and tells him what he has learnt about Deb. Use the verbs below.

refill • not bathe • not use • have

Bob – She .... for ages, you know! It was hard to believe at first.

But she .... quick showers instead of baths, don't worry!

You know what? She .... any plastic bags or aluminium foil

for years! She .... her reusable containers instead.

This girl is incredible, isn't she?

b. Write about something you have been doing for some time to protect the environment. Say how long you've been doing it.

A few ideas

recycle plastic bottles • recycle old papers • print on both sides of sheets of papers...

....

....

....

....

....

3 A NEWSPAPER ARTICLE — Chris Martin in action

◆ Read.

a. Read the text once on page 91 and tick the right answer.

1. The article is about	☐ a pop group and Fair Trade.	☐ a pop group and organic food.
2. The group is	☐ Coldplay.	☐ U2.
3. The lead singer is	☐ Bono.	☐ Chris Martin.

b. Read the text again and correct these sentences by quoting from the text.

1. Chris Martin has been involved in Fair Trade since he went to university.

....

2. He doesn't want to involve his fans in the cause of poor farmers.

....

c. Read once more and answer the following questions.

1. Where has the singer become aware of the disastrous living conditions of farmers in developing countries? ....

2. Who invited him? ....

3. Why can't the farmers earn a living (*gagner leur vie*) in developing countries?

....

4. Who is taking advantage of the situation? How?

....

5. There are dramatic consequences for the farmers and their families. Give 3 examples:

- ....
- ....
- ....

6. What does the singer do to make his fans aware of the situation?

....

d. Pick out the translations in the text.

1. *pays en voie de développement* : ....

2. *récoltes* : ....

3. *par conséquent* :..

4 MAKE IT YOURS

◆ Write.

Write about the experience of Bono, leader of the rock band U2, and say for how long he has done these things. Use the information below.

- (*organize, play*) in several benefit concerts, (*meet*) several influential politicians → 10 years
- (*be*) at the head of DATA (Debt[1] Aid Trade Africa) to eradicate poverty and HIV in Africa → 2002
- (*produce*) clothing in developing countries to provide fair wages[2] for workers → (*meet*) Irish designer

1. debt [det]: *dette* – **2. wage:** salary

....

....

....

....

....

....

....

....

....

....

....

....

1. Read the texts, look at the pictures and fill in the grid.

Names of the charities	Their aim
....	....
....	....
....	....
....	....

Common point of these organizations: they all deal with the problems of .... people.

2. Read again and give examples of:

– environmental problems: ....

....

– health problems: ....

– social problems: ....

3. Write.

Now choose one of the subjects below and write about your experiences.

Subject 1: *Are you interested in the environment?*
Subject 2: *Have you ever helped any charity?*

Use the vocabulary you wrote above.

....

....

....

....

....

....

....

....

....

1. Watch Part I.

a. What type of document is it? ☐ a report. ☐ a film. ☐ a TV series. ☐ an ad.

b. What are these tourists doing?

☐ Restoring furniture (*meubles*).
☐ Swimming in turquoise waters.
☐ Spending their entire time on golden beaches.
☐ Trying to make a difference.

c. Fill in the charity's ID using some of the elements on the right.

CHARITY'S ID

Name of the charity: ....

Address: ....

Founders (*fondateurs*): ....

Type of business: ....

Motivation: ....

....

Country involved: ....

....

- They were moved (*émus*) by people's suffering (*souffrances*).
- Southampton, England
- travel company
- Indonesia
- Adrian and Sarah Yalland
- "Different Travel"
- They want to earn (*gagner*) money.
- Thailand
- Sri Lanka
- It organizes trips that combine an exotic holiday with voluntary work.

d. How much money has the organization invested so far (*jusqu'à présent*)?

.... pounds.

2. Watch Part II.

a. Cross the odd words out to complete this sentence.

These children **won** / **lost** a year of **food** / **lessons** after the **tsunami** / **origami** but they have caught up with their studies at this displacement **hotel** / **school**, run by a local woman in her own home.

b. What does the woman think about the afternoon spent with the children?

Give an adjective. ....

c. Tick the best adjectives to describe the living conditions at the displacement camp (= where people temporarily live after the destruction of their home).

☐ quite comfortable ☐ extremely poor ☐ dilapidated (*délabré*)
☐ unhealthy (*malsain*) ☐ well-equipped

d. Look at Farashi's house and give adjectives that best describe it.

☐ very cramped (*exigu*) ☐ very rudimentary ☐ roomy (= spacious)
☐ uncomfortable ☐ well-equipped ☐ shocking

e. How long have Farashi and her family been living there? ....

Go to the following website and do the activities below:
http://news.bbc.co.uk/cbbcnews/hi/find_out/guides/uk/comic_relief/

1. Comic relief.

Click on "What is Comic relief?" and answer the questions.

a. What is it? ....

b. Its goals: ....

....

2. Red Nose Day, an initiative by Comic Relief.

Click on "What is Red Nose Day?" and answer the questions.

a. What is it? ....

b. When? ....

c. Where? (countries) ....

d. How? (What do people wear?) ....

e. What for? ....

3. How did it start?

Click on "How did it start?" and answer the questions.

a. When? ....

b. By whom? ....

c. Where from? ....

d. Which channel supported the project? ....

4. How is the money shared?

Click on "Where does the cash go?" and answer the questions.

a. How much money is for Africa? .... ; the UK? ....

b. How much has Red Nose Day raised so far? ....

c. Examples of projects: ....

....

....

5. How can you help?

Click on "How can I get involved?" and answer the questions.

a. At school? ....

b. At home? ....

c. On TV? ....

1. Let's play with words!

Form the words whose definitions are given below.

Every answer has the sound [eə] in it, you saw the words either in the list or through Unit 5.

a. ERAC (to feel responsible for): ....

b. EAARW (being conscious of): ....

c. RESAH (to divide something into parts): ....

d. RWAE (to have clothes on) : ....

e. IRAF (free from dishonesty, injustice): ....

2. Word building.

• Give the meaning of the following verbs.

give: .... give up: ....

turn: .... turn on: ....

Observe :

Dans la colonne de droite, les verbes sont suivis d'une postposition. On appelle ces verbes des *phrasal verbs*.

• Le verbe signifie-t-il la même chose avec et sans la postposition ? ☐ oui ☐ non

Conclus :

Les *phrasal verbs* sont des verbes dont la postposition...

☐ modifie la signification du verbe qui la précède.

☐ ne modifie pas la signification du verbe qui la précède.

• Take one word from each box and complete the sentences with the correct phrasal verb.

LOOK TAKE LOOK GO	FOR OFF AFTER UP

a. The plane .... at 2:30.

b. She .... a baby once a week.

c. Prices .... every year!

d. I'm .... my keys!

SOUNDS

1. Let's play bingo with the [eə] and [eɪ] sounds!

64 **Listen to the conversation. You will hear three words with the sound [eɪ] and two words with the sound [eə]. Tick these five words and say bingo!**

wearing	chair	cake
fair	trade	trainers
hair	sustainable	late

2. Listen!

65 **Listen to the following sentences. What is the pronunciation of "have"? Tick the correct column.**

	[hæv]	[əv]	[v]
a. I **have** been interested in organic food for two years, now.			
b. Have you ever helped any charities?			
c. Of course, I **have**.			
d. You have never recycled paper, **have** you?			
e. Centrepoint members **have** helped hundreds of young people.			

3. A hidden message.

Read and write this sentence in English.

[aɪ hævnt həd ə bɑːθ fə eɪdjɪz]

....

66 **1. Lis ces expressions à voix haute et indique la bonne prononciation du *th-* en position initiale. Puis écoute les expressions pour te corriger.**

4 x 0,25 point
...... / 1 point

***Th**is is it!*	☐ [t]	☐ [ð]	*The river **Th**ames is in England.*	☐ [t]	☐ [ð]
***Th**omas!*	☐ [t]	☐ [ð]	*Who's **th**at boy?*	☐ [t]	☐ [ð]

67 **Lis ces phrases à voix haute et indique si *have* est à la forme pleine ou à la forme faible. Puis écoute les phrases pour te corriger.**

2 x 0,5 point
...... / 1 point

	Forme faible	Forme pleine
a. ***Have** you been to Scotland before?*		
b. *I **have** been there once but I haven't been to Ireland yet.*		

68 **Lis ces mots à voix haute et indique s'ils contiennent la diphtongue [eə] ou [eɪ]. Puis écoute-les pour te corriger.**

4 x 0,25 point
...... / 1 point

share	☐ [eə]	☐ [eɪ]	fair	☐ [eə]	☐ [eɪ]
take	☐ [eə]	☐ [eɪ]	sustainable	☐ [eə]	☐ [eɪ]

2. Tu rentres chez toi et il y a du changement ! Parle de ce qui vient d'avoir lieu en utilisant la forme verbale appropriée et *just*.

plant rosebushes • buy a new set of garden furniture • mow the grass

a. ....

b. ....

c. ....

3 x 1 point
...... / 3 points

3. Vous devez recevoir vos cousins ce week-end ! Observe le dessin ci-contre et dis ce qui est fait et ce qui n'est pas encore fait.

wash the dishes • tidy the house • put the groceries in the fridge • cook dinner • do the shopping

a. ....

b. ....

c. ....

d. ....

e. ....

5 x 1 point ...... / 5 points

4. Parle de toi et précise depuis combien de temps…

a. … tu habites dans ta ville ou ton village.

....

b. … tu apprends l'anglais.

....

c. … tu pratiques un sport ou une activité extra-scolaire.

....

3 x 1 point ...... / 3 points

5. Quel est l'équivalent anglais des mots et expressions ci-dessous ?

barrière : ....

panier de basketball : ....

journée portes ouvertes : ....

organiser : ....

planifier : ....

aveugle : ....

malvoyant : ....

s'inscrire : ....

louer : ....

cartouche d'encre : ....

commerce équitable : ....

être conscient de : ....

12 x 0,5 point ...... / 6 points

Pas de problème. C'est moyen. Il faut que je révise.

Total : ...... / 20 points

1 GET READY!

◆ Look and comment.

What is Colin **doing** next week? So **what is** he **going to** do?

→ Observe et réfléchis

1. Next Thursday Colin is presenting his school project.
2. He's going to make a model of the solar system.
3. Look at those black clouds! It's going to rain.

• Dans la phrase 1, la présentation de Colin est prévue, elle ne s'improvise pas au dernier moment. Souligne le groupe verbal.

Il est formé de .... (conjugué au ....) + verbe qui se termine en -............

• Dans la phrase 2, Colin a l'intention de faire une maquette du système solaire. Souligne le groupe verbal.

Il est formé de .... (conjugué au ....) + ... + la préposition « ..... » + verbe non ....

• Dans la phrase 3, il sait quel temps il va faire, il l'a déduit en regardant le ciel. Souligne le groupe verbal.

Il est formé de .... (conjugué au ....) + ... + la préposition « ..... » + verbe non ....

REMEMBER

• Pour dire ce qui est prévu, j'emploie ....

• Pour dire ce que j'ai l'intention de faire, j'emploie ....

• Pour dire ce que je déduis, j'emploie ....

You're going to have a busy week. Say what you're doing or going to do next week. Use the verbs into brackets.

1. Next Monday, I .... (*have*) a Maths test, so this weekend I .... (*revise*).
2. Tomorrow, we .... (*take*) the car to the garage, so we .... (*cycle*) to school every day next week.
3. Next Saturday I .... (*buy*) a present for Emma because I .... (*go*) to her birthday party.
4. I .... (*go*) to the swimming pool this afternoon. The sky is blue: it .... (*be*) a wonderful day.

2 STEP FORWARD!

A. Listen. Why don't you get him a video game?

MP3 **a. Listen to the dialogue once and tick the correct answer.**

Sally and Harry are talking about ☐ a costume party. ☐ a birthday party.
The party is taking place ☐ next weekend. ☐ tomorrow night.

MP3 **b. Listen again and answer the questions.**

1. Are Sally and Harry going to the party? ....
2. What are they bringing? ....
3. What does Sally suggest to buy for Colin? ....
4. What's Harry's problem? ....
5. What is Sally's suggestion? ....

MP3 **c. Listen to Sally and complete.**

– .... him a video game?

– .... one for two?

– I .... you some.

– .... to the shop after school!

→ Observe et réfléchis

• Dans les phrases ci-dessus, Sally fait des .... pour que Harry et elle puissent acheter un cadeau.
Souligne les expressions utilisées et entoure le verbe qui suit.

Après ces expressions, le verbe est .... ou se termine par ....

REMEMBER

Pour faire des suggestions, on peut utiliser les constructions suivantes :

- .... + le verbe .... ?
- .... + le verbe .... ?
- .... + le verbe ....
- .... + le verbe ....!

B. What about you?

You're on holiday and you are making suggestions to your friends. Put the following words into the correct order:

1. don't / some pizza / invite / why / friends / buy / and / we

....

2. could / watch / we / rent / it / and / a video

....

3. the beach / a picnic / let's / and / go / to / have

....

4. about / to / seaside / the / what / cycling

....

3 A DIALOGUE A visit to Kennedy Space Center

A. Before you listen.

Match the pictures with the words below.

○ an astronaut ○ the Earth ○ in orbit ○ launching
○ a rocket ○ a shuttle ○ space ○ the International Space Station

1

2

3

4

5

6

7

8

B. Listen.

a. Colin and Becky are organizing their visit to KSC. Listen to them and tick what they are talking about to prepare their visit.

☐ Rocket Garden
☐ The Shuttle Launch Experience
☐ Space Shop
☐ Astronaut Memorial
☐ Astronaut Encounter
☐ IMAX Theatre
☐ Space Shuttle Plaza
☐ Mission to Mars

b. Listen again and say if the following statements are true (T) or false (F). Justify your answers.

1. Becky is suggesting to start with the visit of Rocket Garden. ☐ T ☐ F

....

2. At Space Shuttle Plaza there is a replica of the shuttle Explorer. ☐ T ☐ F

....

3. Becky loves scary attractions like roller coaster. ☐ T ☐ F

....

4. Colin is going to go shopping at the Space Shop. ☐ T ☐ F

....

5. In the IMAX Theatre, Colin and Becky can see a film about the ISS. ☐ T ☐ F

....

4 MAKE IT YOURS!

Make plans.

Your English teacher is planning a trip to London with your class.
Look at the map below and suggest what to do or visit on your first day in London.

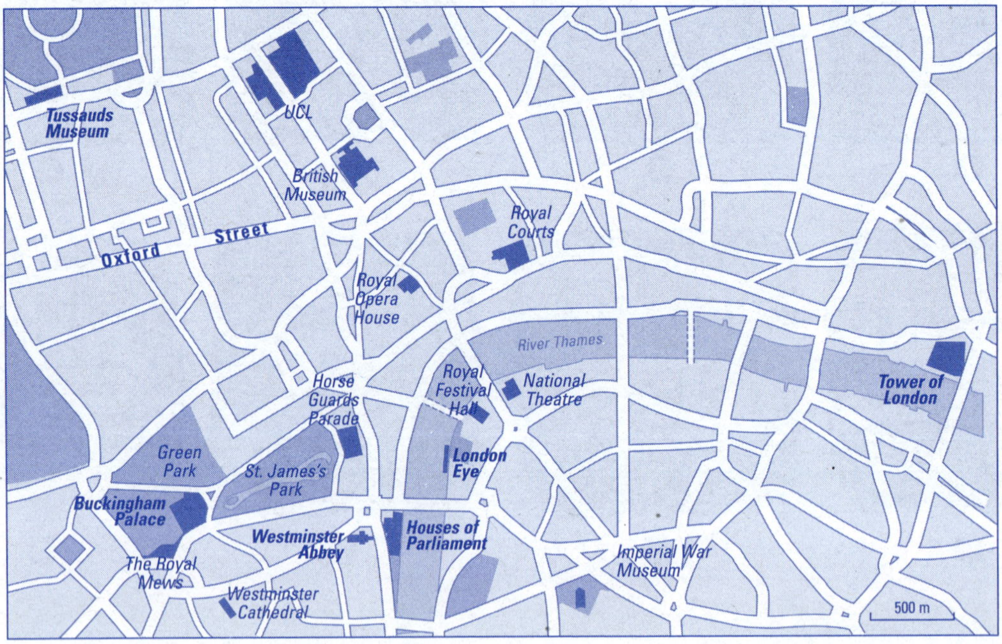

....

....

....

....

1 GET READY!

◆ Look and comment. Innovations **will** change our lives very soon.

You are a salesman and you try to convince someone to build one of these smart houses. Finish the following sentences using the information on the card.

Ex.: *Thanks to solar panels you will save energy.*

1. Thanks to computer-controlled lights ....
....
2. Thanks to a self-cleaning kitchen ....
....
3. Thanks to robots ....
....

> **Make your house a smart home!!!**
> **Let technology make life easier!**
> Solar panels, computer-controlled lights and heating, self-cleaning kitchens, robots...
> Visit us at your nearest shop.

Sounds: [æ] and [ɑː]

Here are two pronunciations of the vowel "-a-"
Ex.: *manager* [æ] *mars* [ɑː]

69

69 **Do you hear [æ] or [ɑː]? Listen to the following words and tick the right pronunciation.**

	parcel	smart	smash	gadget	garbage	dark	factory	fast	camera	cast
[æ]										
[ɑː]										

2 STEP FORWARD!

B. Look and listen. Teachers and pupils **will communicate** via webcam.

70 **a. Listen to the interview of a scientist, Mr Wells, and tick the correct answer.**

1. What is the subject of the interview? ☐ New technologies at school today.
☐ A vision of the school of the future. ☐ An experiment done in England.
2. What will be different according to Mr Wells? ☐ Computers will replace teachers.
☐ Pupils will stay at home to study. ☐ Teachers will go to pupils' houses.

b. Say if the following statements are true (T) or false (F). Justify your answers.

1. Home learning doesn't exist. ☐ T ☐ F
....
2. There will still be teachers. ☐ T ☐ F
....
3. Pupils who won't have a computer will go to school. ☐ T ☐ F
....

c. Give three advantages of home learning.

– ....

– ....

– ....

d. Tick the correct answer.

1. The journalist thinks pupils need ☐ books instead of computers.
☐ school rules.
☐ to meet friends and speak with other kids or adults.

2. According to Mr Wells, as soon as home learning is generalized, pupils will have more...
☐ choice. ☐ autonomy. ☐ work. ☐ significant results. ☐ friends.

→ Observe et réfléchis

1. As soon as every family is equipped, **pupils will have lessons via the Internet.**
2. When they have a question, **they will contact a teacher via the Internet.**

• Entoure en rouge le verbe de la proposition principale (en gras).

À quelle forme verbale est-il ? ....

• Encadre les expressions qui introduisent la subordonnée de temps.
Entoure en bleu le verbe de la subordonnée de temps.

À quel temps est-il ? ....

REMEMBER

• Quand le verbe de la proposition principale est conjugué avec l'auxiliaire .... + base verbale, le verbe de la subordonnée de temps introduite par .... ou par .... est au ....

C. Write.

Things will change in the future. Complete the following sentences, using the verbs below.

look like (ressembler) • *fly* • *not be* • *find* • *replace* • *manage* (réussir) • *cure* • *not go*

1. When cars .... there .... any more traffic jams.
2. Doctors .... cancer as soon as scientists .... a vaccine.
3. Pupils .... to school any more when computers .... teachers.
4. What .... children .... when scientists .... to clone humans ?

3 AN ARTICLE Life in 2050

A. Read.

Read the text in your textbook page 105 and answer the following questions.

a. About the text.

1. This text is ☐ an article. ☐ a letter. ☐ the summary of a book.
2. Where can you find the original text? ....
3. This text was written ☐ in 2050. ☐ after 2050. ☐ before 2050.

b. Holographic Feedback TV.

1. "Virtual reality games are already popular." Can you give an example by quoting the text?

....

2. A hologram is ☐ a 3D image. ☐ a future channel on TV. ☐ a new generation of screen.
3. Today, it is possible to ☐ touch ☐ feed ☐ eat ☐ smell ☐ watch a hologram.
4. In 2050, it will be possible to ☐ touch ☐ feed ☐ eat ☐ smell ☐ watch a hologram.

c. Water.

1. "Demands for water will increase" means that ☐ we will need less water.
   ☐ we will have too much water.
   ☐ we will need more water.
2. What do futurologists think? ☐ We will die because there won't be any water left.
   ☐ People will fight because of water.
   ☐ We will look for water on another planet.

d. Technology: What is the advantage of robots in factories? Tick the correct answer and justify by quoting the text.

☐ They are never tired.

....

☐ They don't need food.

....

☐ They don't need money.

....

☐ They are easily replaceable.

....

B. Listen.

a. Listen to the people interviewed and answer the questions.

1. What is the interview about?

....

....

2. How do these people feel about the future?
Tick the correct column (several answers are possible).

	scared	enthusiastic	hopeful	thrilled	pessimistic
Boy					
Girl					
Old man					

b. Listen again and answer the following questions.

First interview:

1. What device will be improved? ☐ mobiles. ☐ DVD players. ☐ MP3 players.

2. What will be special about them? ....

Second interview:

3. The girl is speaking about the future of ☐ transport. ☐ medicine. ☐ food.
4. She hopes that in the future it will be possible to...
   ☐ cure people. ☐ clone people. ☐ "repair" people.
   ☐ make new humans. ☐ bring the dead back to life.
5. She is afraid that in the future it will be possible to...
   ☐ cure people. ☐ clone people. ☐ "repair" people.
   ☐ make new humans. ☐ bring the dead back to life.

Third interview:

6. What does the old man fear about the future? Complete:

– "There will .... "

– "If not, ... "

7. He thinks scientists should ☐ invent new technologies.
☐ concentrate on the future of the planet.
☐ prepare for the next war.

1 GET READY!

◆ What about you? What can they do?

a. Imagine you are "Superteen". You're answering Spider-Man's questions.

A few ideas

lift a heavy stone • fly high in the sky • go to bed early • save the Universe • keep my identity secret...

SPIDER-MAN – Tell me Superteen, what can or can't you do?

SUPERTEEN – ....

SPIDER-MAN – What about your obligations?

SUPERTEEN – ....

b. Are your parents strict or not? What are you allowed to do or not to do at home? Make sentences.

A few ideas

drink soda and eat snacks • go out at night • listen to music in my bedroom • chat on the net at any time of the day • do my homework in the morning before going to school...

....

....

....

....

2 STEP FORWARD!

A. Listen and comment. I'll be able to ... and won't have to ...

MP3 **a. Listen to this dialogue between a boy and his mother and tick the correct answer.**

1. The dialogue is about
   - ☐ a boy who wants to have superpowers.
   - ☐ a boy who is afraid of spiders.
2. His mother
   - ☐ supports him.
   - ☐ doesn't support him at all.

Step 3

MP3 b. Listen again and tick the right answer in the grid.

	will be able to	won't be able to	will have to	won't have to	will be allowed to	won't be allowed to
stick to solid surfaces						
see in the dark						
do Physics homework						
spend hours doing homework						
be ready to save people						
stay up late						
obey parents						
do stupid things						

→ Observe et réfléchis

1. He'll be able to do his homework very quickly.
2. He won't be able to do French exercises.
3. He'll have to fight evil people.
4. He won't have to wear his costume all day long.
5. He will be allowed to stay up late.
6. He won't be allowed to go out at night.

• À quel moment ces phrases font-elles référence? ☐ au présent ☐ au futur

Relève les trois formes de l'auxiliaire : ....

• Complète le tableau suivant :

	Phrase	Groupe verbal
autorisation	n°	« .... »
interdiction	n°	« .... »
obligation	n°	« .... »
absence d'obligation	n°	« .... »
capacité	n°	« .... »
incapacité	n°	« .... »

REMEMBER

Pour exprimer au futur :

- l'................................, j'utilise l'expression ***will be allowed to*** + base verbale.
- l'interdiction, j'utilise l'expression « .... » + base verbale.
- l'obligation, j'utilise l'expression « .... » + base verbale.
- ...., j'utilise l'expression ***won't have to*** + base verbale.
- ...., j'utilise l'expression ***will be able to*** + base verbale.
- l'incapacité, j'utilise l'expression « .... » + base verbale.

Write about your future. Say what you'll be able to do, what you'll be allowed to do and what you'll have to do when you are 25. You can use "whereas".

A few ideas

vote • get married • live on my own (*seul*) • have a family • have a job...

....

....

....

....

3 A COMIC STRIP Mutants!

A. Read.

a. Read the document and tick the correct answer.

1. What kind of document is it? ☐ a comic strip. ☐ a newspaper article.
2. The old man ☐ has created a school for humans. ☐ has created a school for mutants.

b. Read the document again and say if the following statements are true (T) or false (F). Justify your answers.

1. When they are adults, mutants will be allowed to use their powers whenever they want. ☐ T ☐ F

....

2. When they are adults, mutants will have to leave the Professor's school. ☐ T ☐ F

....

3. They will be accepted by humans as soon as they leave the Professor's school. ☐ T ☐ F

....

c. Match the elements below.

They will not be permitted to •	• use their powers outside the Professor's school.
They will be obliged to •	• control their powers.
They will be permitted to •	• teaching at the Professor's school.
They will be capable of •	• use their powers inside the Professor's school.

d. Using expressions from the text, say in English:

1. Ils n'auront pas le droit d'utiliser leurs livres.

....

2. Ils auront le droit d'utiliser leur ordinateur.

....

3. Par-dessus tout, ils devront être tolérants.

....

4. Ils ne seront pas obligés de venir.

....

5. Ils seront capables de comprendre.

....

6. Ils ne seront pas capables de voir.

....

4 MAKE IT YOURS!

◆ Write.

You read a job offer for a role and you would like to apply. But you don't know how to get ready for the audition. So you go on an Internet forum to ask questions and get informed. What will you have to do? What will you be allowed to?

....

....

....

....

....

....

....

....

....

....

1. History in brief.

Read the first paragraph and say if the following statements are true (T) or false (F). Justify your answers.

a. The first man stepped on the moon in 1961. ☐ T ☐ F

....

b. People have wanted to travel in space for a long time. ☐ T ☐ F

....

c. In the 1960s, the United States and the Soviet Union collaborated to go to the moon. ☐ T ☐ F

....

d. The first man in space was American. ☐ T ☐ F

....

e. The ISS was launched in 1999. ☐ T ☐ F

....

2. Daily life in space.

Read the second paragraph and find out what is different from life on Earth.

....

....

....

....

3. In the future.

Complete these three sentences.

a. NASA will ....

b. People will ....

c. Tourists will ....

1. Watch the video, then tick the correct answers.

a. The presenter is speaking about a station called...
☐ the moon on Earth. ☐ Apollo II. ☐ Mars on Earth. ☐ weekend in Mars.

b. This station will help people learn how to live...
☐ on the Red Planet. ☐ on Earth. ☐ on the moon.

c. The habitat: complete the sentence.

A group of .... and NASA .... are spending the ....
.... two .... inside this habitat.

d. They want to figure out (= understand) how people will live...
☐ in the desert. ☐ on Mars. ☐ in space.

2. Fill in the following ID grids.

FRANK SCHUBERT
Job: ☐ archaeologist ☐ engineer ☐ geologist ☐ architect ☐ mission commander
Station he works for: ....

EPHIMIA MORPHEW
Job: ☐ teacher ☐ mission commander ☐ space psychologist ☐ geologist ☐ architect
She works for the Johnson .... Center in ....
She also works with the .... Space ....

THE CREW
Their mission:
When they leave their habitat, they will have to wear simulation .... and it will take .... to get ready. In the desert they will look for .... life in the surface rocks.
Afterwards, the crew will collect samples (*échantillons*) from their ....
Crew's name: ....

1. Mars, the red planet.

Go to the following website and answer the questions.

http://www.esa.int/esaKIDSen/SEM3L6WJD1E_OurUniverse_0.html

1. Why is Mars called "the red planet"?

2. Which Roman god gave its name to the planet?

3. What's the average temperature on Mars?

2. Life on Mars.

Go to the following website and answer the questions.

http://www.esa.int/esaKIDSen/SEMR09WJD1E_OurUniverse_0.html

1. Why did people think Martians lived on Mars?

2. Have scientists found any sign of life on Mars so far?

3. Future Mars exploration.

Go to the following website and answer the questions.

http://www.esa.int/esaKIDSen/SEM3L6WJD1E_OurUniverse_0.html

1. What problems will the first humans face when they live on Mars?

http://www.esa.int/esaKIDSen/SEM2UIWJD1E_LifeinSpace_0.html

2. Which conditions will be necessary for people to go to Mars?

WORDS

1. Crosswords.

Read the following sentences and complete with a word from the list in your textbook, then tick the words in the word search.

a. The Mission Rocky Rocket is going to land on the ....

b. The President of the United States will be present when NASA .... the .... next week.

c. The .... will be at 12:00 next Wednesday. So, don't miss this special event!

R	T	R	F	Z	H	Y	C	F	H
M	O	O	N	Q	N	P	O	M	D
A	Q	C	D	S	D	S	J	H	F
J	W	K	O	P	P	E	Y	Y	G
P	D	E	P	A	R	T	U	R	E
S	P	T	Z	E	G	F	R	O	F
A	D	Q	C	W	A	O	E	Q	K
V	A	X	A	O	S	O	X	D	Y
T	L	O	H	M	R	T	C	Z	F
I	M	Z	O	A	T	I	B	F	S
U	L	A	U	N	C	H	E	S	T

SOUNDS

1. Listen!

73 Listen to the following words. Do you hear the sound [ɪ] or the sound [iː]? Tick the correct pronunciation.

	[ɪ]	[iː]
sheep		
ship		
sit		
seat		
leek		
lick		
cheeks		
chicks		

2. A hidden message.

Read and write this sentence in English.

[aɪm gəʊɪŋ tə weə ən æstrənɔːt kɒstjuːm]

....

1. Tu veux faire une fête de fin d'année au collège. Fais des suggestions à tes camarades en les formulant de quatre façons différentes.

buy some cakes • decorate the English class • bring some CDs • buy a present for the English teacher

a. ....

b. ....

c. ....

d. ....

4 x 0,5 point
...... / 2 points

2. Tu fais un exposé pour ta classe en présentant ce qui aura changé dans le futur.

cars • food • houses • clothes • school • environment

a. ....

b. ....

c. ....

d. ....

e. ....

5 x 1 point
...... / 5 points

3. Les choses suivantes se réaliseront dans le futur mais quand ? Construis des phrases en utilisant « *when* » ou « *as soon as* ».

a. people live longer / scientists / cure cancer

....

b. cars / cleaner / less pollution

....

c. fewer accidents / cars / safer

....

d. save energy / use / solar panels

....

4 x 1 point
...... / 4 points

4. Quel est l'équivalent anglais des mots et expressions ci-dessous ?

visite guidée : ....

maquette : ....

fusée : ....

navette spatiale : ....

UNIT 6 Let's recap!

OVNI : ....

extra-terrestre : ....

système solaire : ....

panneau solaire : ....

soigner : ....

une BD : ....

être conscient de : ....

usine : ....

12 x 0,25 point
...... / 3 points

5. Tu vas faire un stage sportif et linguistique de quinze jours en Angleterre cet été. Observe le dépliant et explique ce que tu seras capable de faire (ou non), ce qui sera obligatoire (ou non) et ce qui sera autorisé (ou non) en utilisant les expressions données.

	Monday*	Tuesday	Wednesday	Thursday	Friday	Weekend
Morning	English class	English class	English class	English class	English class	
Afternoon	horse-riding or sailing	swimming or surfing	free time	visits to local sites	tennis or golf	

* One Monday every other week, a day in London is organized but not compulsory.

You spend your weekends at your host family.
We remind you that:
– mobile phones are allowed
– smoking is forbidden.
– going out after 9 p.m. is forbidden.

A few ideas

study English • do sport everyday • go out at night • smoke • spend a day in London • spend the weekend on my own

a. ....

b. ....

c. ....

d. ....

e. ....

f. ....

6 x 1 point
...... / 6 points

Pas de problème. C'est moyen. Il faut que je révise.

Total : ...... / 20 points

THE CURIOUS INCIDENT OF THE DOG IN THE NIGHT-TIME

Mark Haddon

A. Global comprehension

a. Who? Pick out the name...

1. ... of the owner of the dog: ....

2. ... of the dog: ....

3. ... of the narrator and his age: ....

b. There are two other people. What are their jobs? ....

c. Where? Tick where the scene takes place.

☐ In Mrs Shears' garden.
☐ In Mrs Shears' house.
☐ In the street.

d. When? Pick out the time of the event.

....

e. What? Correct these statements by quoting the text.

The dog is wounded.

....

Someone killed it with a knife.

....

B. Detailed comprehension

a. Number the events in the chronological order:

The policewoman and Mrs Shears went back home.	....
The police arrived.	....
The policeman touched Christopher.	....
Christopher found Wellington lying on the grass.	....
Mrs Shears ran to her dog screaming.	....
Christopher hit the policeman.	....
The policeman asked Christopher a lot of questions.	....
The policeman's questions made Christopher feel very ill-at-ease*.	....
Christopher started making strange noise.	....

* **ill-at ease:** nervous and embarrassed.

b. Pick out two verbs showing Mrs Shears is very upset.

1. .... 2. ....

c. What's special about Christopher? Pick out three details in the text showing Christopher is not an ordinary boy.

....

....

....

d. The extract is...

☐ ... the beginnining of the story.
☐ ... the end of the story.

LAMB TO THE SLAUGHTER

Roald Dahl

1. Read Part 1 of the short story (from line 1 to line 15) and fill in the grid.

Characters	– .... – ....
Place	....
Time	....

Then tick the correct answers.

a. The woman is buying ☐ potatoes. ☐ beans. ☐ carrots. ☐ peas. ☐ meat. ☐ fruit. ☐ an apple pie. ☐ a cheese cake.

b. Her husband doesn't want to eat out tonight because ☐ it's too late. ☐ he's too tired. ☐ they haven't got any money.

c. The woman doesn't buy meat because
☐ they don't eat meat. ☐ she has cooked some fish. ☐ she has a frozen leg of lamb.

2. Read Part 2 (from line 16 to line 30) and tick the correct answers.

a. Mrs Maloney wants to ☐ go home quickly. ☐ go to the baker's. ☐ cook a good dinner for her husband. ☐ go to the restaurant.

b. She thinks ☐ they will enjoy their evening. ☐ they will have a good meal. ☐ something terrible might happen. ☐ she might have a shock.

c. She says she ☐ must do everything natural. ☐ must be a good actress. ☐ mustn't be frightened. ☐ mustn't act.

d. When she goes back home, she ☐ puts the food in the kitchen. ☐ starts cooking. ☐ finds her husband dead. ☐ brings a drink to her husband.

e. Mrs Maloney ☐ starts crying. ☐ feels happy. ☐ pretends to cry. ☐ shouts.

3. Read Part 3 (from line 31 to line 64) and say if these sentences are true (T) or false (F) and justify by quoting from the text.

a. Mrs Maloney thinks her husband is dead. .... ☐ T ☐ F

b. She immediately runs to her neighbours'. .... ☐ T ☐ F

c. She doesn't know the policemen. .... ☐ T ☐ F

d. She's deeply upset. .... ☐ T ☐ F

e. She's a suspect. .... ☐ T ☐ F

Then fill in the grid about the police investigation.

Mrs Maloney's story (l. 45-46) .... (l. 55-56)	
Clues (l. 46-47)	
Police actions (l. 49-53)	
Police conclusions (l. 59-61)	

4. Read Part 4 (from line 65 to the end) and answer the questions.

a. What's in the oven? ....

b. What does Mrs Maloney want? ....

c. What do the policemen decide? ....

d. What are they talking about during the meal? ....

Now read the last three sentences and answer the questions.

e. "Personally, I think it's right here on the promises." : What does "it" refer to? ....

f. "Probably right under our noses." : What is there under the policemen's noses? ....

g. "And in the other room, Mary Maloney began to giggle." : Why does she react like that? ....

....

5. Express your opinion.

a. Who killed Mr Maloney? ....

b. What was the weapon? ....

c. Why did the murderer kill him? ....

....

6. Read again. Find clues and quote the text.

a. Part 1: Mrs Maloney manipulates the grocer. ....

b. Part 2: She tries to do everything right and natural. ....

c. Part 3: Mrs Maloney manipulates the policemen. ....

d. Part 4: Why does she convince the policemen to eat the meat? ....

30 ph © Alamy / Photo 12.com
Mise en page : Dany Mourain • **Iconographie :** Hatier Illustration • **Cartographie :** Légendes carto (p. 46)
Illustrations : Johanna Crainmark (p. 10c, 11, 21, 23, 24, 45, 48), Dominique Fages (p. 4, 8, 9, 10g, 10d, 41, 50, 51).

PAPIER RECYCLÉ

Achevé d'imprimer en Italie par Grafica Veneta S.p.A. - Trebaseleghe
Dépôt légal : 93052-2/05 - Juin 2011